MINECRAFTER

ARCHITECT

AMAZING STARTER HOMES

D0061588

MEGAN MILLER

Sky Pony Press
New York

Sky Pony Press books may be purchased in bulk at special discounts for sales promotion, corporate gifts, fund-raising, or educational purposes. Special editions can also be created to specifications. For details, contact the Special Sales Department, Sky Pony Press, 307 West 36th Street, 11th Floor, New York, NY 10018 or info@skyhorsepublishing.com.

Sky Pony® is a registered trademark of Skyhorse Publishing, Inc.®, a Delaware corporation.

Minecraft® is a registered trademark of Notch Development AB. The Minecraft game is copyright © Mojang AB.

Visit our website at www.skyponypress.com.

Authors, books, and more at SkyPonyPressBlog.com.

10 9 8 7 6 5 4 3 2 1

Cover and interior art by Megan Miller
Cover design by Brian Peterson

Book design by Megan Miller

Print ISBN: 978-1-5107-3255-1
E-Book ISBN: 978-1-5107-3259-9

Printed in the United States of America

CONTENTS

Introduction   v

1. Forest Hills Hobbit Hole   1

2. Ice Plains Igloos   12

3. Desert Splendor Palace   23

4. Dark Forest Witch's Tower   38

5. Savannah Safari Camp   67

6. Little House on the Plains   80

7. Extreme Hills Llama Ranch   100

8. Mega Taiga Treetops   111

9. What's Next   122

INTRODUCTION

DESIGNING BUILDINGS IS ONE OF THE MOST FUN and rewarding tasks in the game of Minecraft. This beginner's guide will challenge your creativity and help you become an even better Minecraft architect.

I love a good challenge. One challenge I like to give myself when I start a new Minecraft world is to build my starter home, little or big, in the biome where I spawn. It also has to be a complete starter home, not a hole in the ground—unless it's a hobbit hole!

The starter homes in this book are all designed to use the materials and blocks you can easily get in a single biome, whether you spawn there or not. There are also two phases for the building: a first-night phase and a finalizing phase. The first night's builds are quick and use local material that you can gather on your first day. They're made from local trees and

cobble or stone, with windows made of wood fences. This phase will set the groundwork while you get settled and gather more material for the rest of the build. Once you're more established, you can move on to the next phase: finalizing your amazing starter home!

This book also includes blueprint diagrams to help show where blocks, doors, and windows belong. Blueprints are the diagrams that architects use to illustrate where a building's rooms, walls, and features should be placed. They're called blueprints because they used to be printed with white lines on special blue paper.

Different types of diagrams on a blueprint include:

- **Floorplans,** which show the ground-level outline of the building and the location of walls, doors, windows, and other important features.

- **Cross sections,** which are like a slice that's cut from the center of the building.

- **Elevations,** which show the front, back, sides, or top of a building.

Builder's Tip

ALWAYS REMEMBER TO LIGHT UP YOUR BUILDINGS AS YOU GO!

Don't forget to share your finished buildings and unique customizations with me online. You, or a family member, can tweet me at @meganfmiller to showcase your work.

CHAPTER 1
FOREST HILLS HOBBIT HOLE

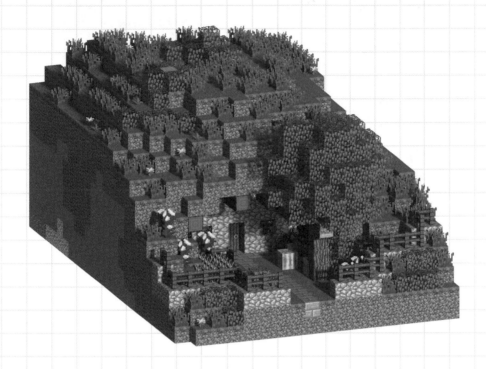

HOBBITS ARE FICTIONAL, DWARF-LIKE CREATURES CREATED BY AUTHOR J. R. R. Tolkien in his books *The Hobbit* and *The Lord of the Rings*. Hobbits live in the countryside in underground or hillside homes called hobbit holes.

Forest and Forest Hills are great biomes for a hobbit hole, as there are lots of hills for digging. And because you simply dig into the ground to make hobbit holes, they are a great starter home. Or, instead of digging into the ground to build your hobbit hole, you can build the basic structure above ground and then cover it in dirt and grass, creating your own custom hills. This design is medium-sized, with a basic template designed to let you easily construct branching tunnels and dig down into the earth. Use the blueprint HH-1 on the next page as a reference as you build.

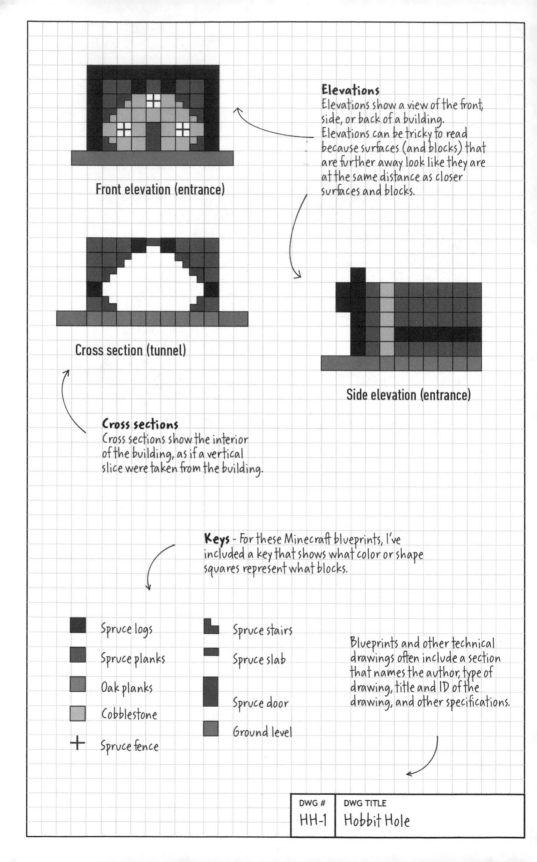

Front elevation (entrance)

Elevations
Elevations show a view of the front, side, or back of a building. Elevations can be tricky to read because surfaces (and blocks) that are further away look like they are at the same distance as closer surfaces and blocks.

Cross section (tunnel)

Side elevation (entrance)

Cross sections
Cross sections show the interior of the building, as if a vertical slice were taken from the building.

Keys - For these Minecraft blueprints, I've included a key that shows what color or shape squares represent what blocks.

Spruce logs
Spruce planks
Oak planks
Cobblestone
+ Spruce fence

Spruce stairs
Spruce slab
Spruce door
Ground level

Blueprints and other technical drawings often include a section that names the author, type of drawing, title and ID of the drawing, and other specifications.

DWG #	DWG TITLE
HH-1	Hobbit Hole

First Night Directions

1. Dig a 9x6 opening into the hillside of your choice. This will make the hobbit hole deep enough to fit your bed and chest. The opening should be 1 block below ground level so you can add your own floor blocks.

2. Use cobblestone for the front wall. Place your spruce door and spruce fence windows, as shown. Inside, add oak planks for flooring. Your hobbit hole will look cozier and more hidden if your entrance way is placed a few blocks into the hill. However, you can always add more "hill"—dirt and grass—to the front later.

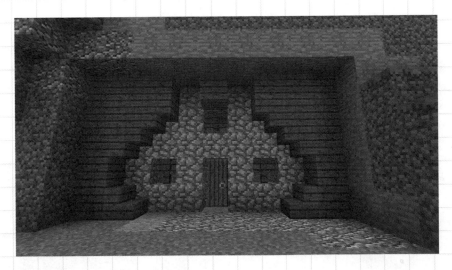

Finishing the Hobbit Hole

3. For the entrance, first place spruce blocks and stairs in front of the cobble wall, as shown. Refer to blueprint HH-1 (page 2) for a view of the front, sides, and a cross section of the hobbit hole.

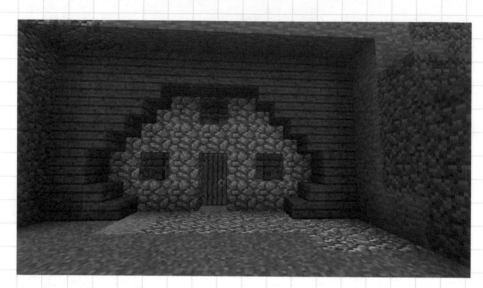

4. Add support beams of spruce log on the sides and above the top layer of spruce planks, as shown. You may have to remove some stone or dirt to place the top beam.

5. Add 4 support beams of spruce log extending out from the existing beams by 2 blocks, as shown.

6. Now add dirt above the support beams and to the sides of the vertical support beams. This will make the hobbit hole look like it's hidden deeper inside the hill.

7. Inside, continue digging out your 9x6 tunnel. Continue as far as you want into the hill.

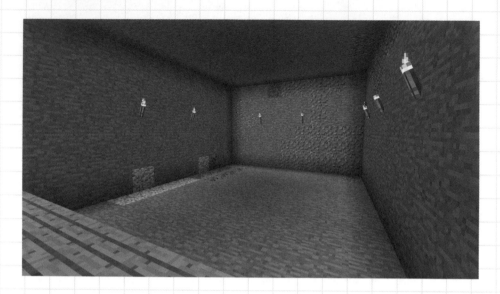

8. Copy the pattern of spruce logs, spruce planks, spruce slabs, and spruce stairs in blueprint HH-1 (page 2) to set up your tunnel walls (and floor).

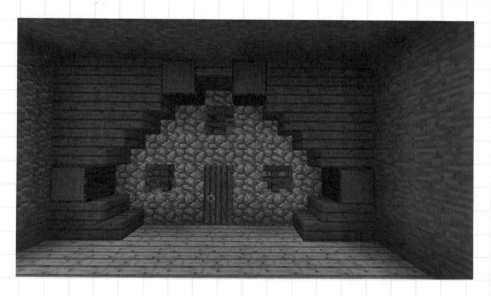

9. Continue this pattern all the way to the end of your tunnel.

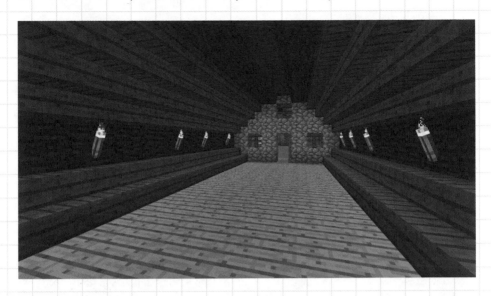

10. At the end of the tunnel, use spruce planks and logs to construct the back wall.

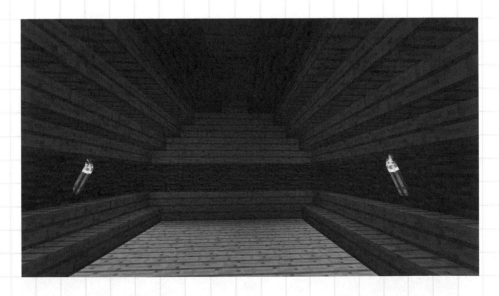

11. Round out the back wall by adding spruce stairs at the same levels of the side walls.

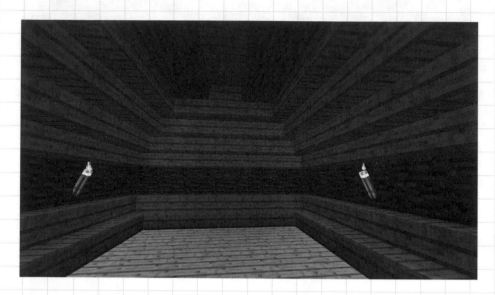

Building Tunnels

12. To make tunnels that branch off your main tunnel, you can copy the pattern you've already used. First, cut out the 9x6 hole where the tunnel will go, and make the tunnel as deep as you like.

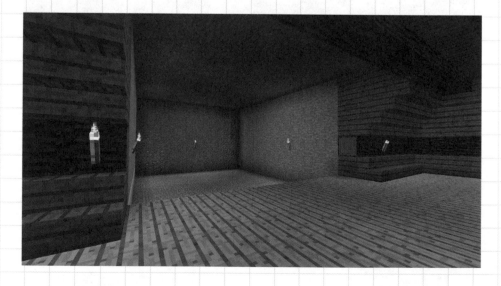

13. Use the same pattern for floor, walls, and ceiling to round out the tunnel.

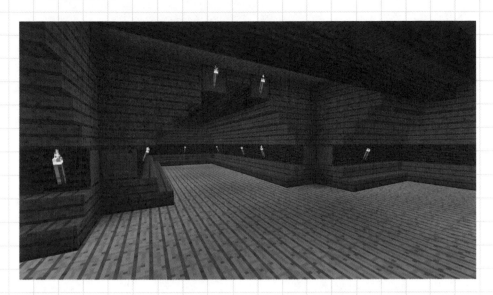

14. There are a number of ways to round out the corners between the adjoining tunnels. Here I've used spruce log "support beams" and spruce stairs at the top and bottom.

Creative Add-ons

Digging Down

You can also run these tunnels further underground. Instead of your 9x6 tunnel running straight, step the tunnel down 1 block every 2 or 3 blocks.

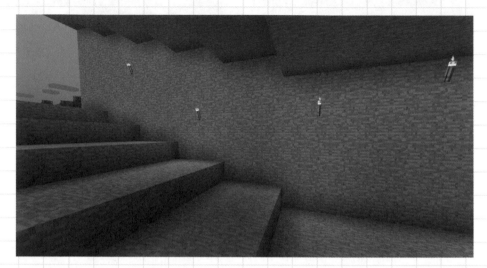

Once you've stepped down the excavation as far as you like, repeat the wall, floor, and ceiling pattern for each segment. Use oak stairs to step down to each next level.

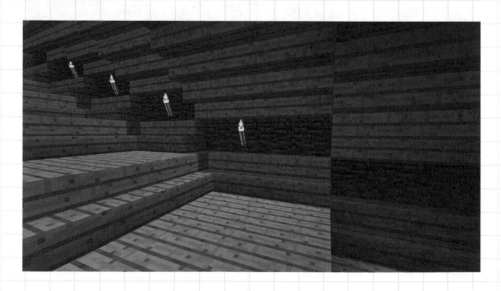

Man-Made Hill Building

You can also use this wall, ceiling, and floor pattern to create your hobbit hole above ground, without excavating a hill. You can then cover the structure with dirt and plants to make a custom hill. With a custom hill, you can arrange it so that there are places where you can add additional entrances and windows.

CHAPTER 2
ICE PLAINS IGLOOS

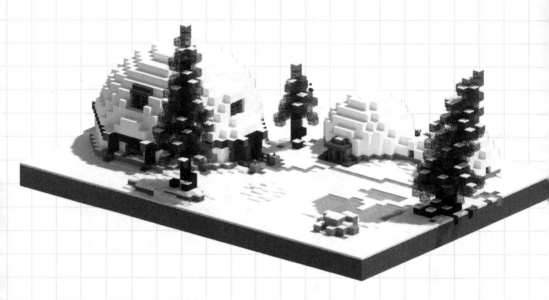

THE ICE PLAINS MAY SEEM LIKE AN UNFORGIVING terrain in which to spawn, but you can live there successfully, even if it is a bit more difficult than plains living. There aren't a lot of trees, or a lot of animals, but there are enough resources to survive. Spruce wood and snowy rabbits can keep you alive. Just keep your distance from polar cubs, so as not to aggravate their mothers. You can grow crops here, but you will need water. Place torches around ice to melt it so that you can water the crops. These directions will show you how to make both igloos in the igloo compound: the Ice Plains igloo and the Ice Plains Chief's igloo.

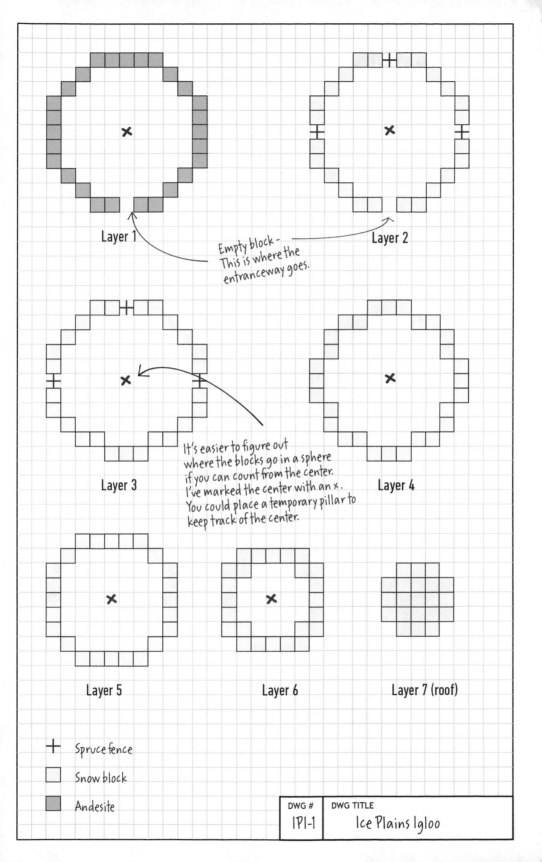

Layer 1

Layer 2

Empty block -
This is where the
entranceway goes.

Layer 3

It's easier to figure out
where the blocks go in a sphere
if you can count from the center.
I've marked the center with an x.
You could place a temporary pillar to
keep track of the center.

Layer 4

Layer 5

Layer 6

Layer 7 (roof)

✛ Spruce fence

☐ Snow block

▨ Andesite

DWG #	DWG TITLE
1PI-1	Ice Plains Igloo

First Night Directions

1. Build the circular base for your igloo out of andesite blocks. (If you don't have andesite yet, use cobblestone.) Follow the blueprint for placing the blocks for Layer 1. Then remove a layer of snow blocks inside the igloo and add spruce slabs for flooring.

2. Build the next 6 layers to complete the dome of the igloo, using snow blocks and spruce fence for the windows. Add a temporary spruce door to use until you finish the entranceway.

Builder's Tip

YOU MAY WANT TO FENCE IN YOUR WORKING AREA WHEN WORKING IN THE ICE PLAINS BIOME TO KEEP CUBS (AND DANGER) AWAY.

Finishing the Igloo

3. For the entranceway, first add 5 andesite blocks around the door opening, as shown.

4. Place 2 spruce stairs on either side of the top andesite block.

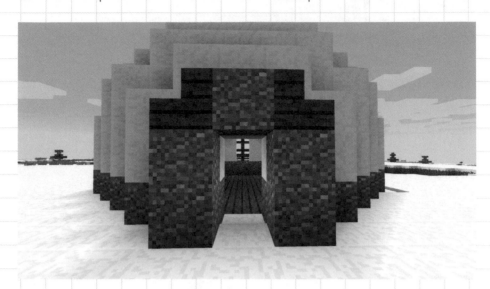

5. In front of the top andesite block and spruce stairs, place 3 spruce slabs to finish the entranceway roof. Add 2 spruce fences on each side as support.

6. Add 8 andesite as the entranceway floor, as shown.

7. Finally, add a spruce door 1 block in.

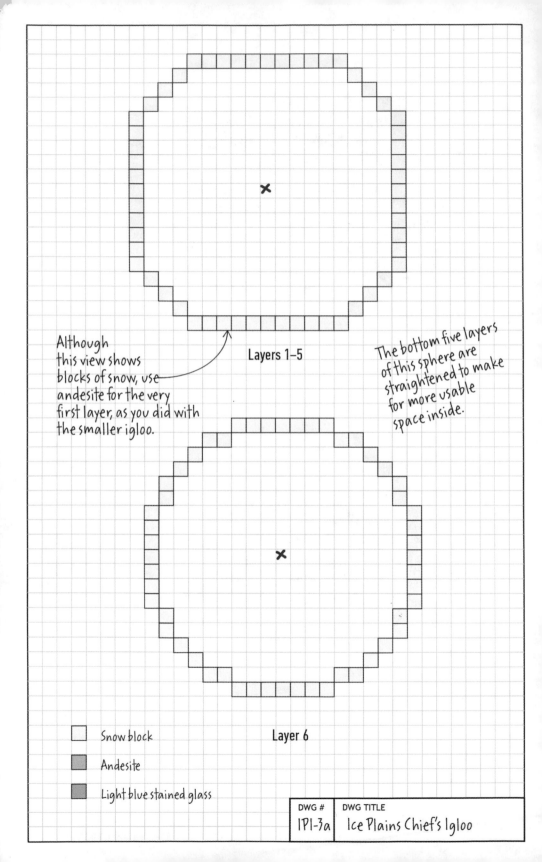

Layers 1–5

Although
this view shows
blocks of snow, use
andesite for the very
first layer, as you did with
the smaller igloo.

The bottom five layers
of this sphere are
straightened to make
for more usable
space inside.

Layer 6

☐ Snow block

▨ Andesite

▨ Light blue stained glass

DWG #	DWG TITLE
1P1-3a	Ice Plains Chief's Igloo

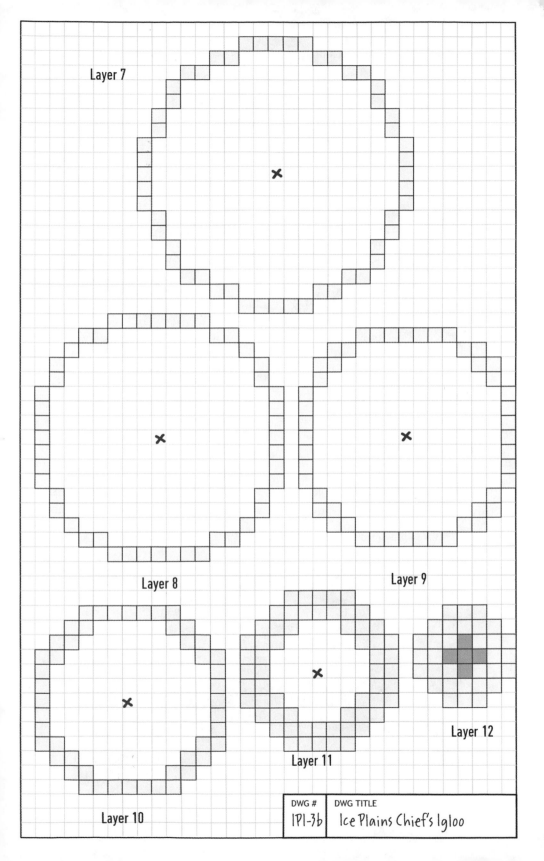

Layer 7

Layer 8

Layer 9

Layer 10

Layer 11

Layer 12

DWG #	DWG TITLE
IPI-3b	Ice Plains Chief's Igloo

Chief's Igloo Directions

9. Use blueprints IPI-3a and IPI-3b to (pages 18 and 19) create the base sphere for the second igloo—the chief's igloo. It will be much larger than your first igloo.

Creative Add-ons

Passageways

You can build a larger complex of igloos using the base igloo design and adding snow-block passageways between them, like the one shown on the blueprints to follow. Refer to blueprint IPI-2 at right for the shape of the passageway.

Passageway Blueprint

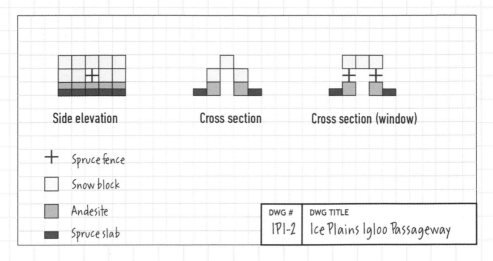

Side elevation   Cross section   Cross section (window)

+   Spruce fence

☐   Snow block

▨   Andesite

▬   Spruce slab

DWG #	DWG TITLE
IPI-2	Ice Plains Igloo Passageway

Interior Details

Inside, I've added a loft area supported by spruce beams and staircases of andesite and spruce. Windows are made of spruce fence and spruce stairs.

Exterior Details

Use andesite, spruce logs, planks, slabs, and fences to detail your chief's hut. Outside, I've replaced some snow blocks with spruce logs to look like support all around the building. I've added an entryway with andesite, spruce fence, and spruce doors, and added extra snow on top of the spruce beams. I've made windows of spruce fence as well.

Enjoy your new igloo compound!

CHAPTER 3
DESERT SPLENDOR PALACE

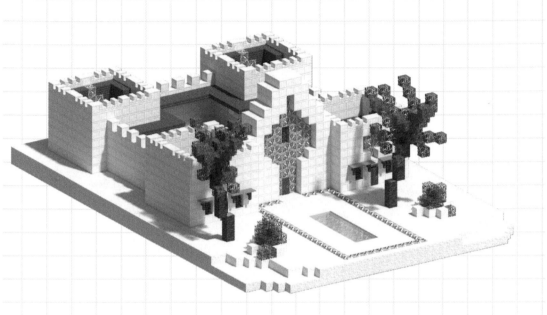

LIKE ICE PLAINS, DESERT IS A MORE CHALLENGING biome in which to set up camp. You will need to bring some items that you can't find in the desert, including seeds, trees, and some dirt. You might also want to bring along some animals. Desert bunnies are the exception. For wood, I recommend spruce, as that contrasts very nicely with sandstone. With all the hardship in setting up your food resources, you may as well live it up in style in a small desert palace! This palace has a central, open courtyard, and walls decorated with patterned terracotta.

First Night Directions

1. Build a 9x9 square using smooth sandstone.

2. Add 6 more levels of smooth sandstone so that the walls are 7 blocks high.

3. On the front wall, add a spruce door. On either side, add 2 windows using spruce fence, as shown.

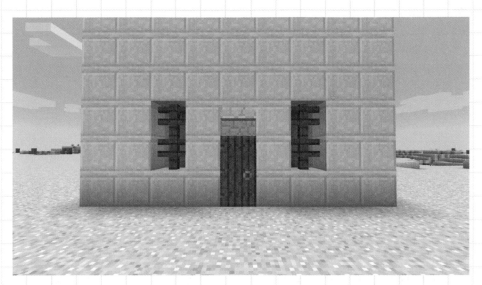

4. Inside, use spruce wood planks as the floor and as a ceiling. Leave 4 blocks between the floor and ceiling.

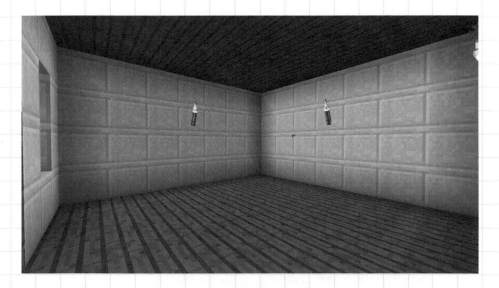

Finishing the Palace

5. First, we'll finish up the first tower of the palace. Add a ladder up to the ceiling at the back right of the tower.

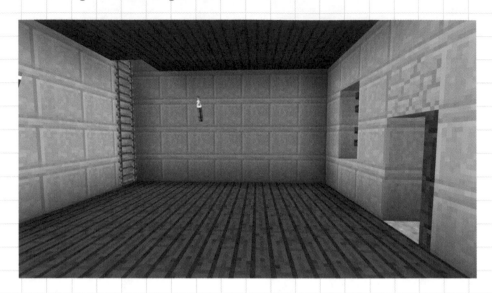

6. On the ceiling, place 8 smooth sandstone blocks: 1 at each corner and 1 above the center of each wall, as shown.

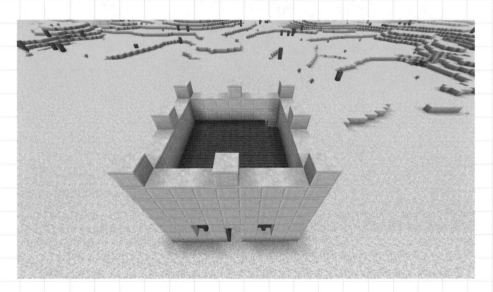

7. Between one of the centered blocks and a corner block, place a row of 3 sandstone stairs. Place the stairs so that their backs are toward the centered block.

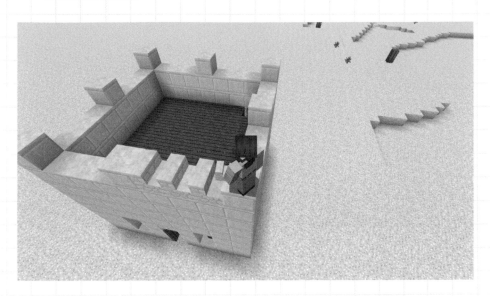

8. Repeat this pattern for the other 7 sections of the roof walls.

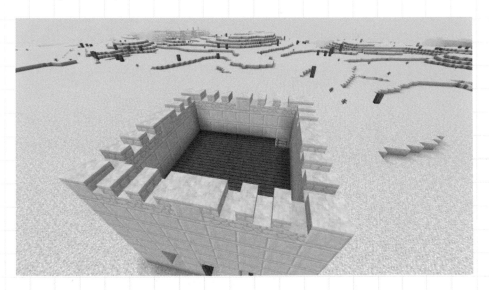

9. On the front wall of the tower, break a hole that is 4 blocks tall and 1 block wide, above the door, as shown. Then on either side of this opening, break another 2 blocks, as shown.

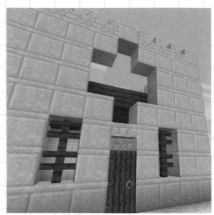

10. On the other side of the hole, place orange-glazed terracotta blocks in the same shape, so that they cover the hole. They should be placed 1 block back from the hole, as shown. You will need to break a few spruce planks in the ceiling to do this. When you are done, replace any holes in the ceiling.

11. Add a 2-block-high lookout run along the side and front walls using spruce planks and spruce stairways.

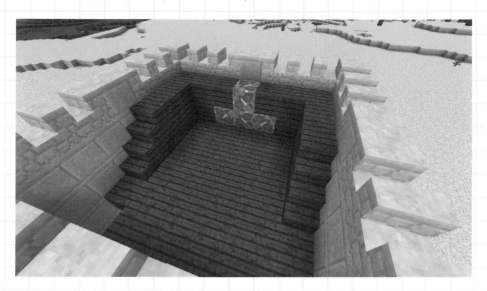

12. Now we'll create awnings for the windows on the front wall. Place 2 spruce fence on either side of a window. In between the 2 fences, place 1 string. Above the 2 spruce fence and the string, place 3 cyan carpet.

13. Do this for the second window as well. Now that the first tower is complete, you can start on the rest of the palace.

14. First, you'll want to replicate this tower 3 more times. The towers will be 11 blocks apart from each other. To help place them, create an 11x11 square of any block, with its front right corner diagonally adjacent to the back left corner of your tower, as shown. Each tower will be placed so that its innermost corner touches this guide.

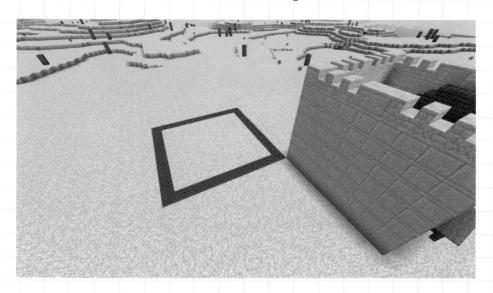

15. The second tower, the front left tower, should have its back right corner diagonal from the guide square, as shown.

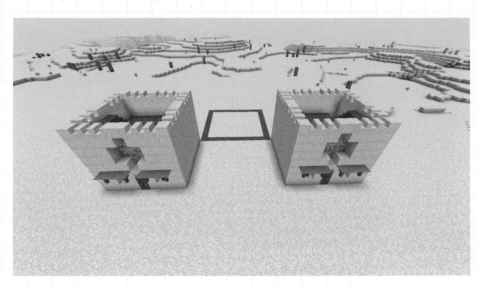

16. Build the last 2 towers with their doors facing backward.

Building the Entrance and Adding Protection

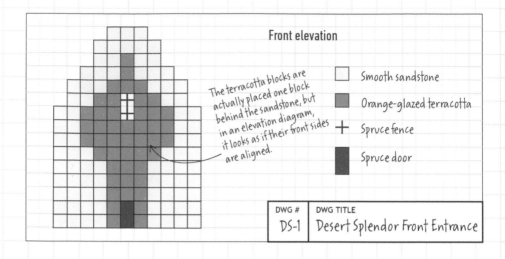

Front elevation

The terracotta blocks are actually placed one block behind the sandstone, but in an elevation diagram, it looks as if their front sides are aligned.

☐ Smooth sandstone

▦ Orange-glazed terracotta

✚ Spruce fence

▬ Spruce door

DWG #	DWG TITLE
DS-1	Desert Splendor Front Entrance

17. Use the blueprint DS-1 to build the outer layer wall of the palace's grand entrance, 2 blocks in from the outer tower walls.

18. Place orange-glazed terracotta blocks, 1 block in from the outer layer, to cover the top portion of the entranceway, as shown.

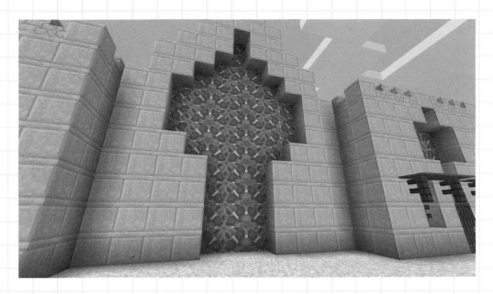

19. In from the terracotta layer, build an exact duplicate of the outer layer of the entrance. This will sandwich the terracotta layer between the outer and inner layers of the entrance.

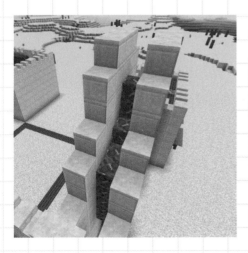

20. Fill in the empty spaces in the inner terracotta layer with smooth sandstone. Add enough so that its height matches the inner and outer layers.

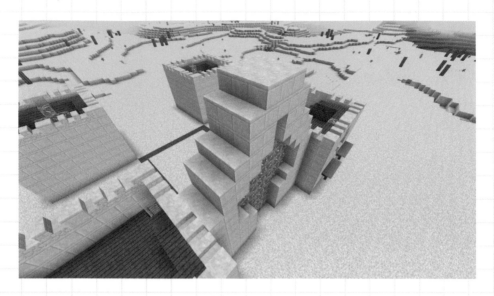

21. Add a spruce door and a spruce-fence window to the entrance, as shown.

22. On the other 3 sides of the palace complex, add smooth sandstone walls. The walls are 2 blocks in from the outer tower walls, and they are 5 blocks tall.

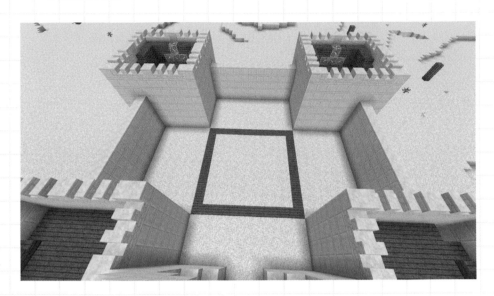

23. Add blocks of smooth sandstone every other block on top of these walls, for added protection from enemies (also called crenellation). The shape and form of your palace are complete.

Creative Add-ons

Interior details

You can add interior decoration, details, doors, and more to make your Desert Splendor home unique.

Here are some items to consider adding:

- Sandstone floors, with borders of light-blue, glazed terracotta and spruce planks

- A simple, central fountain

- Spruce slabs for runs along the walls

- Doors to reach the towers from the interior courtyard

Exterior details

Outside, consider adding a shallow, tiled, reflecting pool. You can also build 2 custom palm trees like the ones in the image for added shade using jungle logs and jungle leaves.

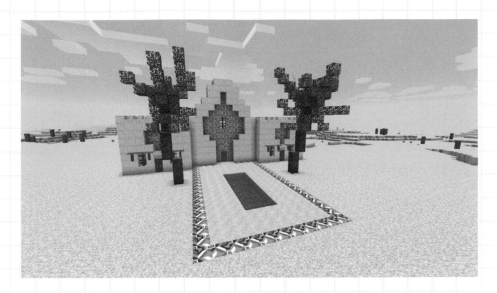

CHAPTER 4
DARK FOREST WITCH'S TOWER

THE DARK FOREST BIOME WITH ITS ROOF of dark oaks is perfect for a witch's or wizard's home. There's quick access to the giant red mushroom, a key resource for brewing potions of weakness and slowness and harming. A tall tower is also useful in the roofed forest, as it lets you look out above the treetops for a glimpse of sunlight.

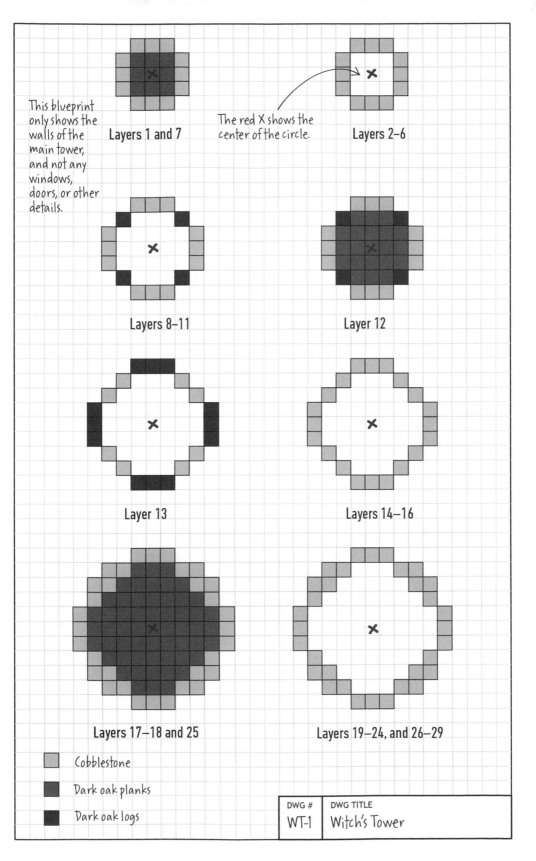

This blueprint only shows the walls of the main tower, and not any windows, doors, or other details.

Layers 1 and 7

The red X shows the center of the circle.

Layers 2–6

Layers 8–11

Layer 12

Layer 13

Layers 14–16

Layers 17–18 and 25

Layers 19–24, and 26–29

Cobblestone

Dark oak planks

Dark oak logs

DWG #	DWG TITLE
WT-1	Witch's Tower

First Night Directions

1. Build a 3x3 floor of dark oak planks and add a 3-block-long base for walls on each side.

2. Build up these walls to be 7 blocks tall, total. Fill in the top of the first level with dark oak planks for a roof.

Good Lighting is a Lifesaver

THE ROOFED FOREST CAN BE A DANGEROUS PLACE TO BUILD. THE TREETOPS CAN BLOCK OUT THE SUN, MAKING IT DARK ENOUGH FOR MOBS TO SPAWN DURING THE DAY. BE SURE TO LIGHT UP THE FOREST AROUND YOUR HOME.

3. Add a dark oak door at the front, and in front of this, add 1 dark oak plank and 1 cobblestone stair.

Finishing the Central Witch's Tower

Second Floor

4. First, place ladders on the back wall to get up to the ceiling. On the top of this floor, add 4 more 3-block-long walls, a block out from the walls beneath. In each corner, add a dark oak log. (As you build this central tower, you can also refer to the blueprint WT-1 on page 39, which shows the blocks to place at each layer for the walls of the towers.)

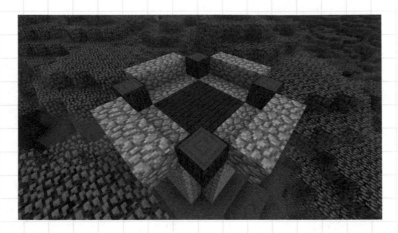

5. Build these walls up to be 5 blocks tall, total. Fill in the top with a floor of dark oak planks. Leave a space at the back to allow for ladders between the first and second floor.

Third Floor

6. Use spruce logs, placed sideways, to add 3-block-long walls, 1 block out from the walls below, on each side of the tower.

7. To connect the side walls, place 2 diagonal cobble blocks at each corner. These are each a block out from the walls below. Then follow this pattern, but use cobble only, to build these walls up to 4 blocks high total.

8. Above these walls, place the 3-block-long sidewalls of cobble, again a block out from the lower walls.

9. Connect these 4 sidewalls with 4 "corners," each made of 3 diagonally placed blocks of cobble, also a block out from the lower walls.

10. Add 2 blocks of cobble to each diagonal "corner," as shown, to make a kind of M shape at each corner.

11. Build this wall up to be 2 blocks high.

Fourth Floor

12. Fill the interior of the top 2 layers with dark oak planks to create a 2-block-thick floor. This is the fourth floor.

13. Bring the ladder up from the third floor.

14. Now add 6 layers to the cobblestone walls, to make them a total of 8 blocks tall, as seen from the outside.

Fifth and Sixth Floors

15. Fill the top layer in with dark oak planks to create the fifth floor.

16. To get from the fourth floor to the sixth floor, build a new ladder along one of the cobblestone "corners."

17. Build the same outer cobble walls up another 5 blocks. Now it is time to start on the roof!

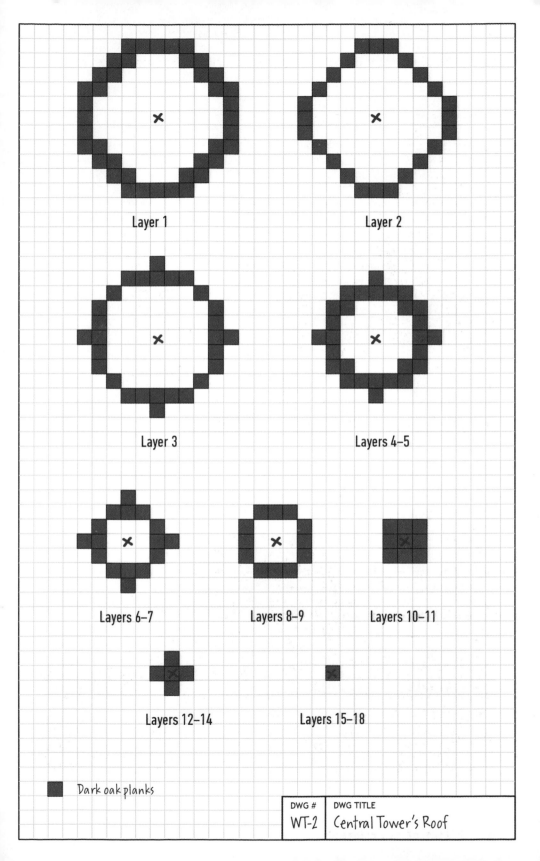

Layer 1

Layer 2

Layer 3

Layers 4–5

Layers 6–7

Layers 8–9

Layers 10–11

Layers 12–14

Layers 15–18

Dark oak planks

DWG #	DWG TITLE
WT-2	Central Tower's Roof

Building the Central Tower Roof

18. Use the blueprint WT-2 on the previous page to build the roof. Use dark oak planks and build 1 layer at a time. Some layers are exactly the same, and each layer is centered above the layer below. The straight sides of roof layer 1 are directly on top of the straight sides of the cobble wall you built in Step 17.

19. To finish off the roof, add dark oak stairs around the bottom layer of the roof.

Building the Second Tower

20. To begin building the lowest of the 2 branched towers, go to the third floor of the tower. Break a 2-block-high hole in the left wall (left as you face the building's bottom front door) and above the dark oak timber. This will be the entrance to the second tower.

21. Outside of this entrance, place a platform of cobble that is 3 blocks wide and extends 4 blocks out from the center tower wall.

22. One block up from this platform, add another platform that is 3 blocks wide and 2 blocks long.

23. Add a 1-block-long strip of cobblestone above the outermost blocks of the platform you built in Step 22.

24. Add a third 3-block-wide "step" that diagonal to the cobblestone you placed in Step 23, as shown. This will be the base of the leftmost wall of the second tower.

25. Build the base of the other 3 walls of the tower, in a Minecraft "circle." Each side is 3 blocks long, and there is a space instead of a block at each corner, as shown.

26. Build the 4 walls up to be 3 blocks tall, total.

AVOID TAKING DAMAGE

WHEN YOU ARE WORKING ON TALL BUILDINGS IN SURVIVAL MODE, PROTECT YOURSELF WITH BOOTS ENCHANTED WITH FEATHER FALLING. THE HIGHER THE FEATHER FALLING ENCHANTMENT ON YOUR BOOTS, THE MORE DAMAGE YOU WON'T TAKE IF YOU STEP OFF YOUR BUILDING OR SCAFFOLDING BY ACCIDENT. ARMOR ENCHANTED WITH PROTECTION WILL ALSO HELP PROTECT YOU FROM DAMAGE.

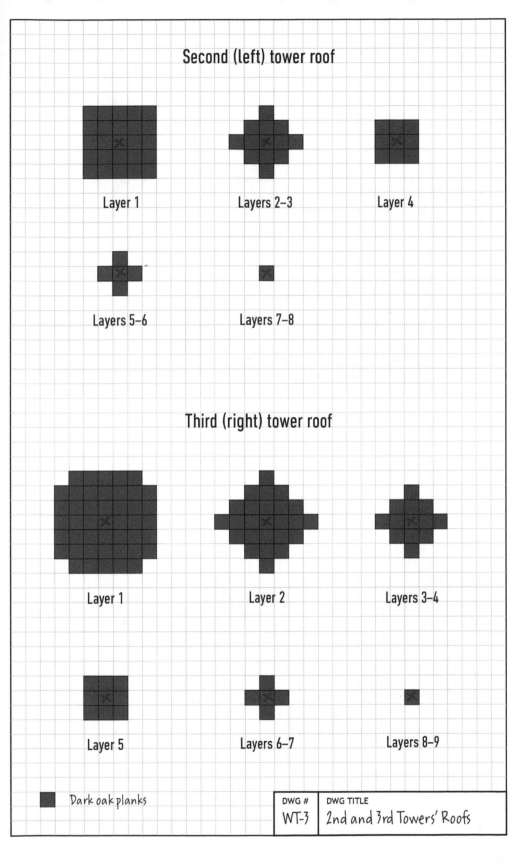

Second (left) tower roof

Layer 1

Layers 2–3

Layer 4

Layers 5–6

Layers 7–8

Third (right) tower roof

Layer 1

Layer 2

Layers 3–4

Layer 5

Layers 6–7

Layers 8–9

Dark oak planks

DWG #	DWG TITLE
WT-3	2nd and 3rd Towers' Roofs

Building the Second and Third Tower Roofs

27. Use the blueprint WT-3 on the previous page to create the 8 layers of the second tower's roof, using dark oak planks.

28. On each side of the first, bottom layer of the roof, place 3 dark oak stairs.

29. On each side of the second layer of the roof, place 2 dark oak stairs. They should face away from the center block along that side, as shown.

30. Now use cobblestone to add walls and a roof to the platform that extends to the tower.

31. To finish off the shape of the second tower, add cobblestone below the platform you built in Step 21 and against the left wall of the main tower. First place a layer that is 3 blocks wide and 3 blocks long. Below that, place just a 3-block-wide and 1-block-long layer of cobblestone.

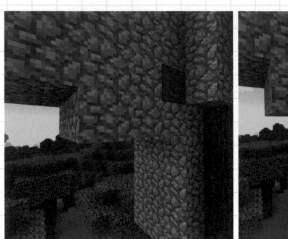

32. Let's build the final, third tower. On the fourth floor, break a 2 block tall entrance along the right wall. Just as you did before, build a series 3-block wide platforms. The first is 6 blocks long, the second is 2 blocks long, and the last is 1 block long.

33. Up 1 block diagonally from the last platform, build the base of the third tower's right wall. It is 3 blocks wide, like the platform.

34. Finish the base of the tower's walls. Each side is 3 blocks long, and there is a diagonal block between each side, as shown.

35. Build up the walls to be 6 blocks tall, total.

36. Use blueprint WT-3 on page 55 to create the roof, 1 layer at a time, using dark oak planks.

37. On each side of the bottom layer of the roof, centered, place 3 dark oak stairs.

38. On each side of the platform extending to the tower, add 2-block-high walls and a 1-block-wide roof of cobblestone, as shown.

39. Inside the tower, fill in each of the 2 areas open to the outside with 3 cobblestone, as shown.

40. Now we need to make the underneath of the platform extending to the third tower look a little more curved. Right below the platform, and against the right wall of the main tower, add a 1-block-thick layer of cobblestone that is 3 blocks long and 3 wide.

41. Below this layer, add a layer that is 2 blocks long (and 3 blocks wide).

42. The base of the third tower, on the front and back, extends out from the base platform by 2 blocks. To make this angle more curved, add a row of 3 cobblestone beneath the tower floor on both the front and back sides.

Creative Add-ons

Windows and Stairs

Now the shape and form of your witch's tower is done, and it's time to add details, like windows! Add the details you like, or follow what I've done. I've added windows on each floor using dark oak fence instead of glass, because to me it looks more medieval. Where there's room, I've added dark oak stairs above and below the window for more detail.

Support Beams

Next I've added dark oak logs to look like support. I've added them below and above the 2 platforms leading to the second and third towers. I've replaced 4 corners on the main and third towers with vertical beams of dark oak. I've also added some dark oak logs below the third and fourth floors to look like they are supporting these floors. Finally, I've added horizontal beams below the walls of the second, smallest tower.

More Add-ons

Other details you may want to add include:

- Mossy cobblestone in place of the regular cobblestone, for a weathered look

- Banners—for an eye-catching salute to potions and witches

- Vines to creep around the towers

- Weathered paths leading to and from your spot in the forest, made of cobblestone, gravel, and stone bricks

- Tiny farms to supply you with your potion ingredients

CHAPTER 5
SAVANNAH SAFARI CAMP

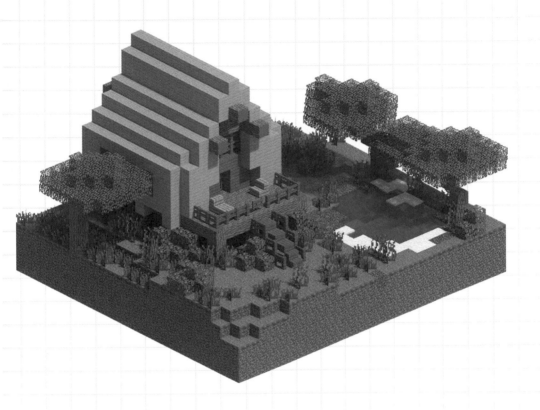

I HAD NEVER REALLY WANTED TO SET UP home base in the savannah, because the grass and trees are dry and gray. I prefer the vibrant, green grass in the jungle. However, I changed my mind when I began thinking of this biome as an exciting African savannah, where I could go on safari photographing elephants and giraffes. This camp design is a semi-permanent tent, where you can sit on your raised porch and watch the wild pigs and buffalo graze near a watering hole. The "fabric" of the camp tent itself does need a fair amount of gray wool, so the walls of your first night shelter will be temporary until you can get the wool.

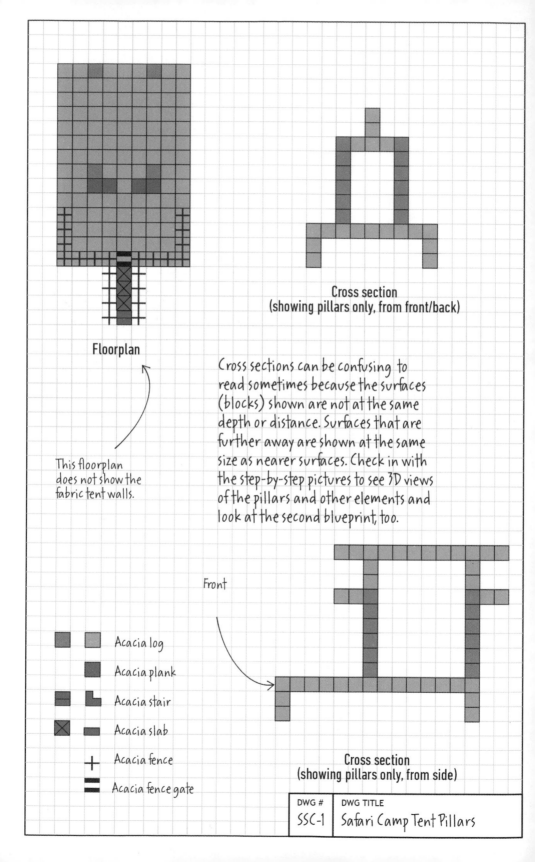

Floorplan

This floorplan does not show the fabric tent walls.

Cross section
(showing pillars only, from front/back)

Cross sections can be confusing to read sometimes because the surfaces (blocks) shown are not at the same depth or distance. Surfaces that are further away are shown at the same size as nearer surfaces. Check in with the step-by-step pictures to see 3D views of the pillars and other elements and look at the second blueprint, too.

Front

Acacia log

Acacia plank

Acacia stair

Acacia slab

Acacia fence

Acacia fence gate

Cross section
(showing pillars only, from side)

DWG #	DWG TITLE
SSC-1	Safari Camp Tent Pillars

First night directions

1. Build a sturdy 14-block-long by 9-block-wide base for your tent from acacia logs. It should look like a large table with 2-block-high legs. One of the short sides will be the porch, so try to point this west for the sunset and/or toward a watering hole.

 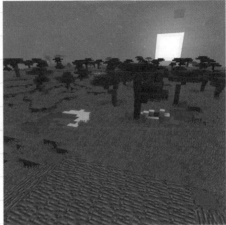

Be on the Lookout for Llamas! ——

IF YOU CHOOSE A SAVANNAH PLATEAU TO PITCH YOUR CAMP, YOU MAY ALSO SEE THE RARE SAVANNAH LLAMA.

2. Add the 4 vertical support beams for your future tent walls. Use the blueprint SSC-1 (page 68) for their exact placement.

3. Add the front wall of the camp, using acacia planks, in front of the 2 frontmost support columns. Add an acacia door in the center.

4. Build walls and a ceiling for the rest of your temporary shelter, using any blocks.

5. Build a stair up to the camp platform using 3 acacia slabs and one acacia staircase, as shown.

6. Add acacia fencing to each side of the stairs, as shown.

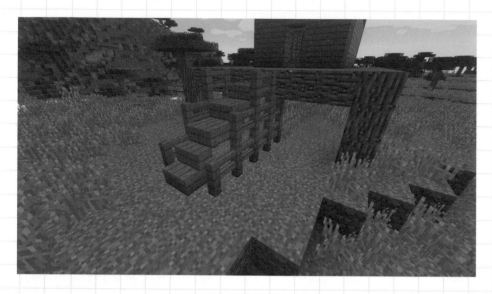

Finishing the Savannah Safari Camp

7. Remove the temporary side and back walls. Add 2 rows of acacia fences above the front acacia wall.

8. Add a pair of 3-block-long beams over each side of the fence, extending out from the front vertical support beams.

9. Add a 3-block-long beam of acacia logs directly above the acacia fences, between the 2 vertical front support beams.

10. Add another 3-block-long beam of acacia logs between the 2 back support beams.

11. Add a pair of 2-block-long beams of acacia log extending back from the 2 back support beams.

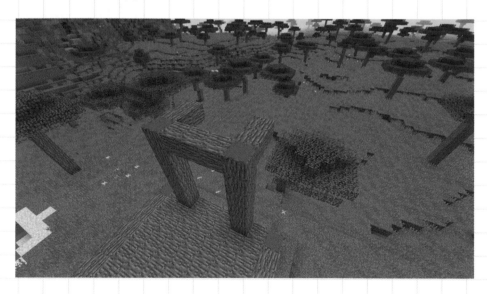

12. Add 2 single blocks of acacia log above the center of the back and front horizontal beams.

13. Run a 10-block-long beam of acacia logs between the 2 support beams you added in Step 12.

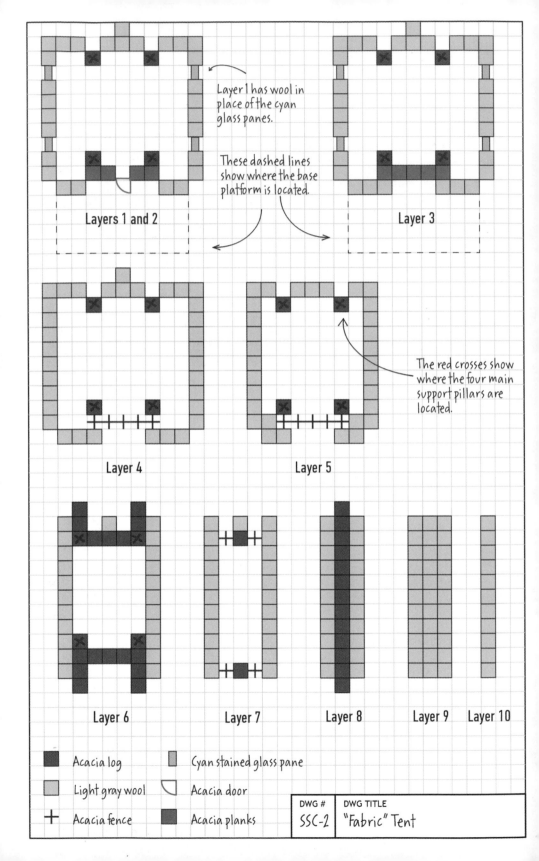

Layer 1 has wool in place of the cyan glass panes.

These dashed lines show where the base platform is located.

Layers 1 and 2

Layer 3

The red crosses show where the four main support pillars are located.

Layer 4

Layer 5

Layer 6

Layer 7

Layer 8

Layer 9

Layer 10

Acacia log

Light gray wool

Acacia fence

Cyan stained glass pane

Acacia door

Acacia planks

DWG #	DWG TITLE
SSC-2	"Fabric" Tent

Creating the Fabric Tent

14. Follow the blueprint SSC-2 on the previous page to place the blocks for the fabric tent that is draped over the support beams. Layer 1 begins the block above the acacia log platform.

15. Notice that, on the second and third layers, cyan stained-glass panes serve as plastic tent windows. Also notice that, on the seventh layer, you will be adding two, 1-block acacia fence windows at the front and back of the tent.

16. Add 4 blocks of wool at the bottom of the tent on each side, as shown. Connect these to the ground with acacia fence, to look like the tent walls are being strapped down with ropes for stability.

17. In the same manner, add 1 block of wool at the back of the tent, too, in the center, as shown. Strap this tent flap to the ground also with a "rope" of acacia fence.

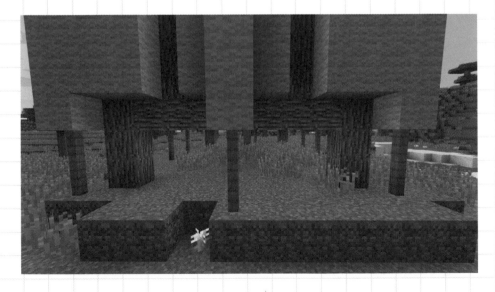

18. Add acacia fencing and a gate to your porch, and you're done! All that's left are your own touches and details. I've added some oak stairs and slabs to relax on while I watch the llamas graze.

CHAPTER 6
LITTLE HOUSE ON THE PLAINS

THE PLAINS BIOME IS ONE OF THE EASIEST biomes in which to start out. There are plenty of animals, flat land to build on and farm, and no shortage of trees. This build is inspired by the home described by author Laura Ingalls Wilder in her *Little House on the Prairie* book series. There's a shed-like building to the right to start off in, and a larger home with a sleeping loft you can build once you have more materials. In the plains, expanding is easy—there's plenty of open land for adding animal pens, barns, and more!

First Night Directions

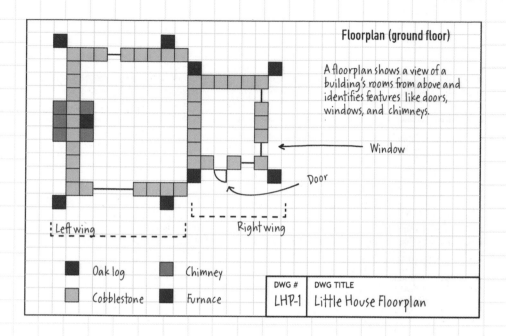

Floorplan (ground floor)

A floorplan shows a view of a building's rooms from above and identifies features like doors, windows, and chimneys.

← Window

Door

Left wing

Right wing

■ Oak log   ■ Chimney
□ Cobblestone   ■ Furnace

DWG #	DWG TITLE
LHP-1	Little House Floorplan

1. Build a simple shelter to keep you safe for your first days on the plains while you gather more materials. Create a 1-block-high rectangle of cobblestone, 6 blocks wide and 7 blocks long. This will be part of the foundation.

2. On the right-hand side of the cobblestone foundation, place 2 columns of oak logs, 4 blocks high. These should be placed diagonally to the 2 corners. You can also see where these are placed in the blueprint LHP-1 on the previous page.

3. On the left-hand side, place 2 columns of oak logs, 5 blocks high. These should be placed alongside the outer edge (back and front) of the cobble rectangle.

4. Continue building the walls by adding 2 rows of oak planks above the cobblestone base.

5. We'll build the shed roof from 3 steps of oak slabs. The first 2, lowest steps are 3 blocks wide each. The top, leftmost step is 4 blocks wide. Place the first step of slabs so that it extends to the right of the oak columns by 1 block. This step, and the next 2, should extend out from the front and back wall by 2 blocks. This step should be a half block below the top of the rightmost columns, as shown. Let the tops of the oak columns show through.

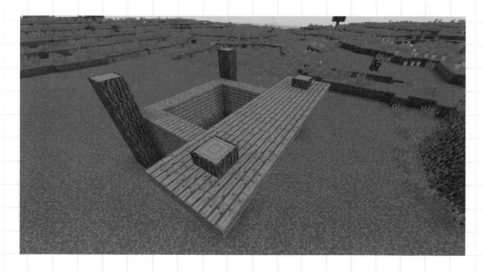

6. Place the next step of oak slabs so that it overlaps the first by 1 block.

7. Place the last step of oak slabs, 4 slabs wide, so that it also overlaps the previous step by 1 block. The left-most slab should align with the left oak columns.

8. Use slabs and full oak plank blocks to fill in the tops of the oak plank walls so that they reach the roof.

9. Add an oak door and a window using oak fence to the front of the shelter.

10. Add 2 windows using oak fence on the right wall.

Finishing the Little House

11. When you are ready to expand, first add a cobblestone base for 3 new walls to the left of the shelter. The front and back walls are 9 blocks long and should start 1 block diagonally out from the right wing's left oak columns, as shown. The left wall is 11 blocks long.

12. Build the 3 walls up with 4 layers of oak wood planks.

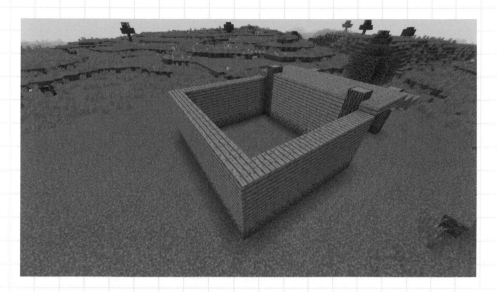

13. One block below the top level of the wall, add a floor of oak planks. This will be the attic floor.

14. Diagonal to the left front and left back corners of the building, place 2 columns of oak logs, 6 blocks tall.

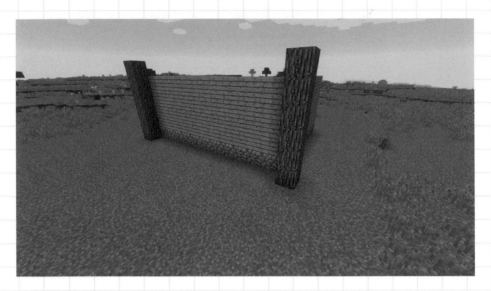

15. One block in from the front right corner of the new building, place another 6-block-tall column of oak log.

16. Place a fourth 6-block-tall oak log column in the same position on the back wall.

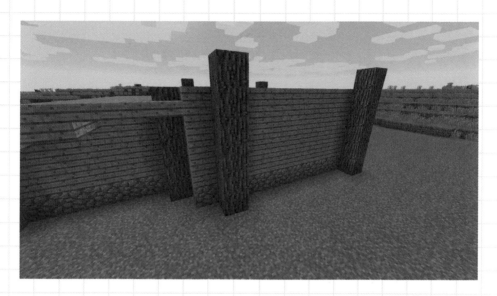

17. Start building the roof of the new building. On the left side, stretching from front to back, add a row of oak stairs. The row should extend 1 block beyond the oak log columns.

18. Add 4 more rows of staircases, each diagonally up 1 from the last. Leave the oak log columns in place, so that they jut through the roof.

19. Do the same for the right side of the roof: Add the bottom row, just 1 block below the top of the oak columns. You will need to replace 2 oak plank blocks with oak staircases as you go. However, leave the oak log columns in place as before, to jut through the roof.

20. Add another 4 rows of oak staircases, as shown.

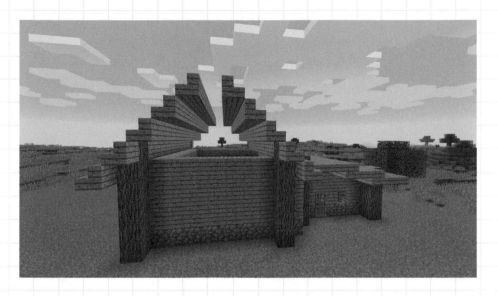

21. Place a row of oak plank blocks between the 2 top rows of staircases, as shown.

22. Finish the peak of the roof by adding a row of oak slabs above the oak plank blocks.

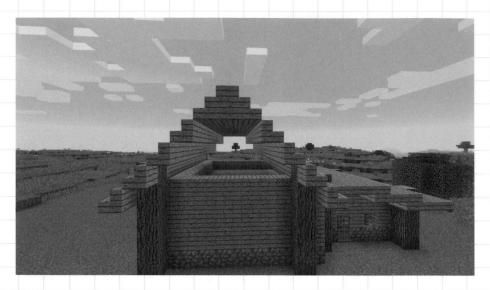

23. Add oak plank blocks to the front and back walls so that they reach the roof.

24. Finish off the roof by adding upside-down stairs just inside the existing oak stairs (and just on the outside of the house).

25. You'll only need to add 1 upside-down stair on the bottom (first) rows. On the second through fourth rows of the roof, you'll need to add 2 upside-down stairs for each row. Do this for the back of the roof as well.

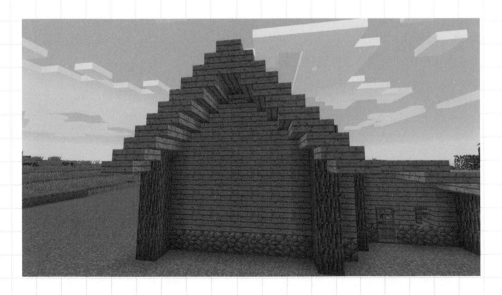

Adding Windows

26. Add a centered, front window that is 3 blocks wide and 2 high, using oak fence instead of glass. Add a row of 3 cobblestone stairs above the window.

27. Above the cobblestone, add a horizontal beam of oak log, and above this, a single block window, as shown.

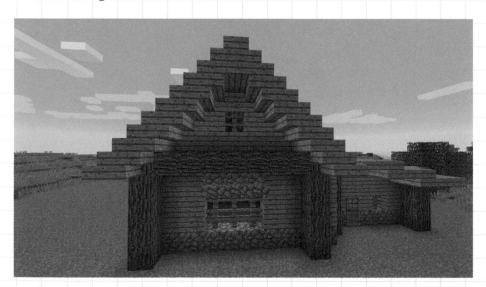

28. On the back of the house, add a 2-block-high window on the bottom floor, a beam of oak wood, and a top window, as shown.

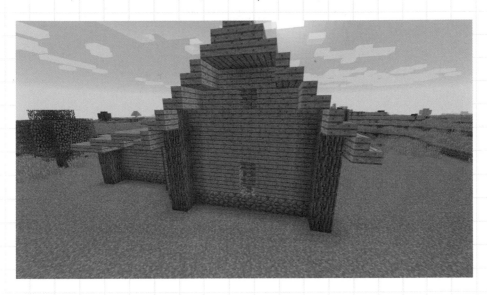

Craft Your Chimney

29. On the left side of the house, add a large chimney made of cobble. Use 6 blocks for the base (2 rows of 3 cobblestone). Add 8 blocks for the column (you'll need to break a roof block to get through). Join the base and column of the chimney with 2 cobblestone stairs.

30. Use cobwebs (use shears to get these from mineshafts) to add what looks like "smoke" to the top of the chimney.

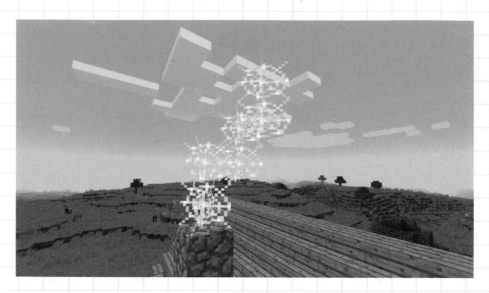

Plains Biome Plusses

THE PLAINS BIOME IS A POPULAR LOCATION FOR BASES FOR ALL OF THESE REASONS:

- EASY TO BUILD ON THIS FLAT LAND
- OFTEN HAS VILLAGES
- A NATURAL SPAWNING POINT FOR HORSES AND DONKEYS
- PASSIVE MOBS ARE COMMON
- THE LACK OF SHADE MEANS THAT MOST ZOMBIES AND SKELETONS WILL BURN AWAY EACH DAWN

Creative Add-Ons

Exterior Details

31. Add a planter outside the front window, made of coarse dirt, oak trapdoors, and your favorite plant or flower.

32. Add a porch roof to your front door made of 6 cobblestone slabs. Support the roof with 2 pillars of cobblestone wall.

Interior Details

33. Inside you'll need to add floors of oak (or spruce) planks. Break a doorway from the right wing of the house to enter the left wing.

34. In the left wing, complete the front of the fireplace with a furnace, cobblestone blocks, and cobblestone stairs.

35. Finally, add a ladder, in the center of the back wall, to get to the attic floor.

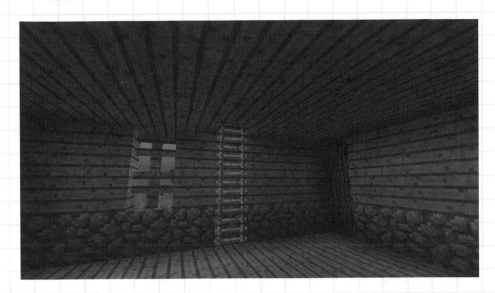

CHAPTER 7
EXTREME HILLS LLAMA RANCH

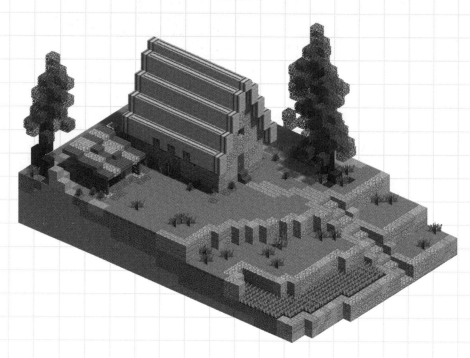

THIS FARMHOUSE IS BASED ON THE FARM and storage houses built by the Incas in Machu Picchu, Peru, high in the Andes Mountains. They are tall, narrow houses with thatched roofs.

What makes this build especially interesting (aside from the llamas) is how the land in the Extreme Hills allows you to farm on a steep mountain slope. The landforms in this biome are based on the ones created by the Inca Empire in the 16th century. The Incans created a gradual series of steps down steep mountainsides so that they could farm more easily. They bordered the flat steps of land (also know as terraces) with stone walls that would absorb the sun's heat and keep the ground warm during cold nights.

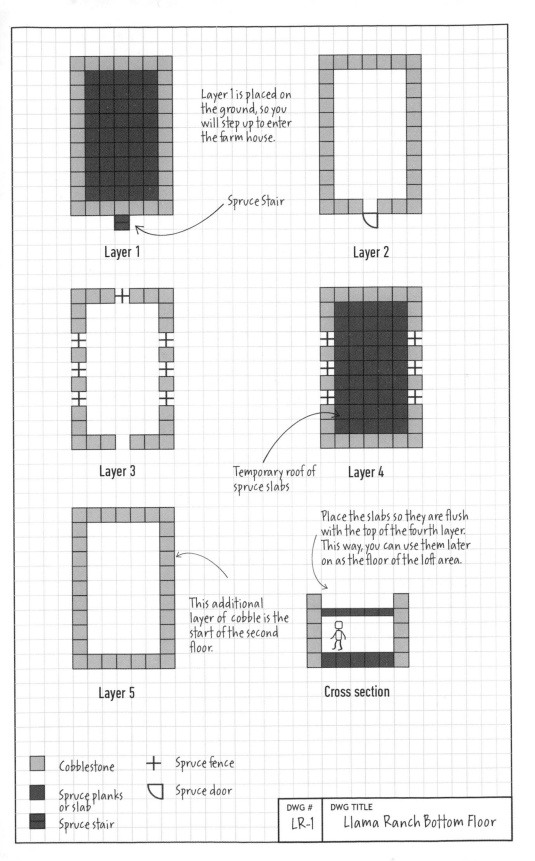

Layer 1 is placed on the ground, so you will step up to enter the farm house.

Spruce Stair

Layer 1

Layer 2

Layer 3

Temporary roof of spruce slabs

Layer 4

Place the slabs so they are flush with the top of the fourth layer. This way, you can use them later on as the floor of the loft area.

This additional layer of cobble is the start of the second floor.

Layer 5

Cross section

Cobblestone

Spruce planks or slab

Spruce stair

Spruce fence

Spruce door

DWG #	DWG TITLE
LR-1	Llama Ranch Bottom Floor

First Night Directions

1. Build the ground floor of the house following the blueprint LR-1 on the previous page using regular cobble and spruce wood. Place the first layer on top of the ground.

2. As the blueprint suggests, use slabs for a temporary roof. You can use these later for the sleeping loft inside of the house.

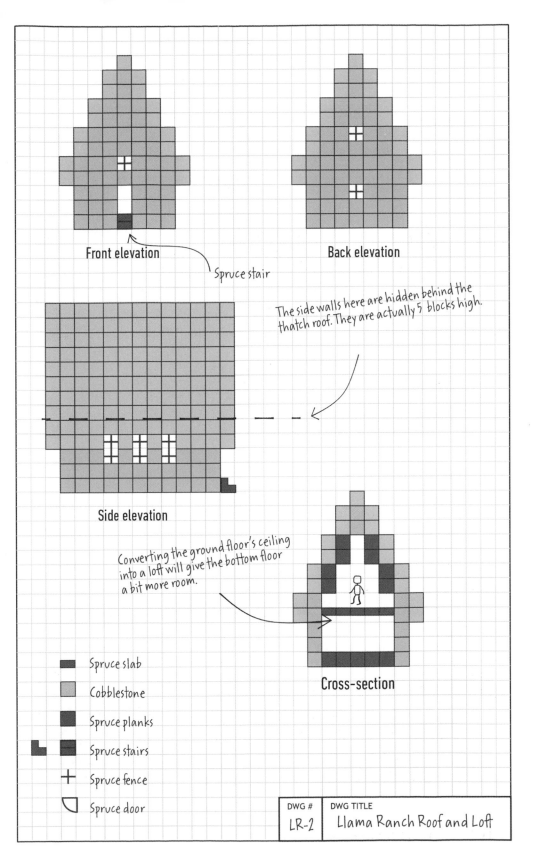

Front elevation

Back elevation

Spruce stair

The side walls here are hidden behind the thatch roof. They are actually 5 blocks high.

Side elevation

Converting the ground floor's ceiling into a loft will give the bottom floor a bit more room.

Cross-section

	Spruce slab
	Cobblestone
	Spruce planks
	Spruce stairs
+	Spruce fence
	Spruce door

DWG #	DWG TITLE
LR-2	Llama Ranch Roof and Loft

Finalizing the Farmhouse

3. Finish the cobblestone walls of the farmhouse, using the front and back elevations on the blueprint LR-2. (An elevation, in an architectural drawing, typically shows the front or sides of a building.)

4. Run a 2-block-high strip of cobblestone from the front to the back walls, as shown.

5. On each side of the house, run 2 additional 2-block-high strips of spruce wood, as shown.

6. Use hay blocks to roof your farmhouse. The roof has 5 steps, as you can see in the blueprint. The bottom 4 rows on each side are 2 blocks high. Extend each row of the hay blocks 1 block out from the front and back walls. Leave the sidewall windows uncovered.

Fun Fact

7. Inside the house, add a ladder to the second floor.

8. You can keep the second floor as it is, or break the front 5 rows of slabs and add a spruce fence to create a sleeping loft. This gives the front of the house a more open feeling.

9. When you have the resources, replace two-thirds or so of the cobble with cracked stone brick and andesite. Add just a few blocks of gravel and regular stone brick. Adding these a bit randomly will make the walls look old and weathered, as if they have been repaired with different stones over the years.

Crafting Terraces

10. To create your tiered farms, Inca style, you will need to create flat tables of land down the mountainside. Starting at the top, where you want your terraces to begin, make the 2 top layers of grass the same shape. Follow the curve of the mountain as best you can.

11. Border this terrace with stone—a mix of cracked stone brick, cobblestone, andesite, and a little gravel.

12. Repeat this all the way down the mountain. You will have to add quite a bit of dirt to keep making each 2-block-high terrace at least 3 blocks wide, including the stone border. You will also find that lower terraces overhang the actual edge of the mountain. You can either fill these gaps in with more dirt, or light them up so that mobs don't spawn.

13. When you are done terracing, carve a 2-block-wide staircase up to the top of the mountain where your farmhouse is. Use cobble slabs and blocks for the stairs and border the staircase with cracked stone.

14. If you wish to use the terraces as farms for potatoes or other crops, you can use the blocks beneath the stone borders to place water blocks to water the crops. You can then cover up the strip of water with your border stones to hide it.

CHAPTER 8
MEGA TAIGA TREETOPS

THE RARE MEGA TAIGA BIOME, WITH ITS GIANT spruce trees, is a great place to set up a peaceful compound of tree huts. You can even join them together with "rope" bridges and add huts at different levels for a unique living experience!

This design includes a blueprint for a small hut, a larger hut, a rope bridge, and a rope bridge entrance. You may want to plan your hut locations in advance using the larger hut as a central focus, with smaller huts branching off. This design also works well for a jungle treetop camp—simply use jungle logs and planks (or any other wood of course) instead of spruce.

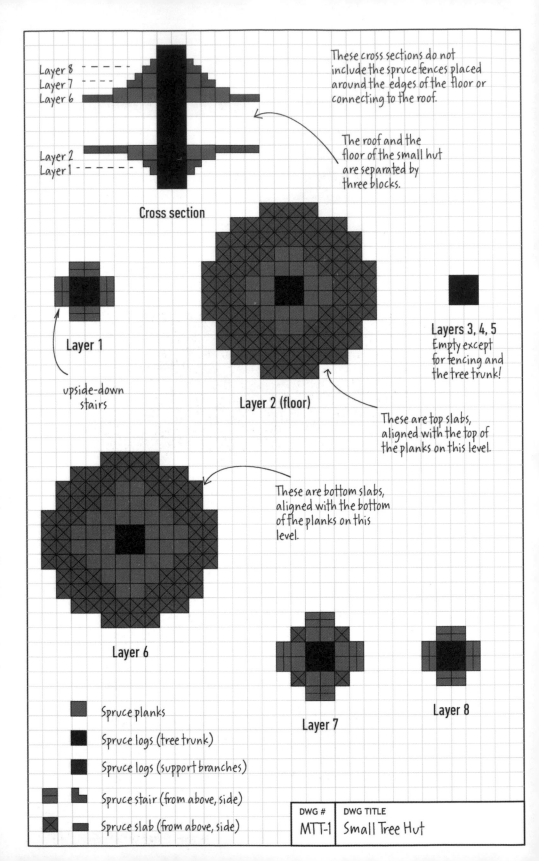

Layer 8
Layer 7
Layer 6

These cross sections do not include the spruce fences placed around the edges of the floor or connecting to the roof.

Layer 2
Layer 1

The roof and the floor of the small hut are separated by three blocks.

Cross section

Layer 1

upside-down stairs

Layer 2 (floor)

Layers 3, 4, 5
Empty except for fencing and the tree trunk!

These are top slabs, aligned with the top of the planks on this level.

These are bottom slabs, aligned with the bottom of the planks on this level.

Layer 6

Layer 7

Layer 8

Spruce planks

Spruce logs (tree trunk)

Spruce logs (support branches)

Spruce stair (from above, side)

Spruce slab (from above, side)

DWG #	DWG TITLE
MTT-1	Small Tree Hut

First Night Directions

1. Use the blueprint MTT-1 on the previous page to build your first small treetop hut. Plan so that the floor is 12 blocks above the ground. This will make it easy later to create your first rope entry bridge. In the meantime, use a ladder to reach the level you want, place a few slabs around you, and get started! Run spruce fencing around the sides, and add columns of spruce fence on each side of the platform "circle's" sides, as shown.

Finalizing the Treetop Village

2. Build a rope bridge entry, using the blueprint MTT-2 on the next page. On either side of the bridge, add spruce fences.

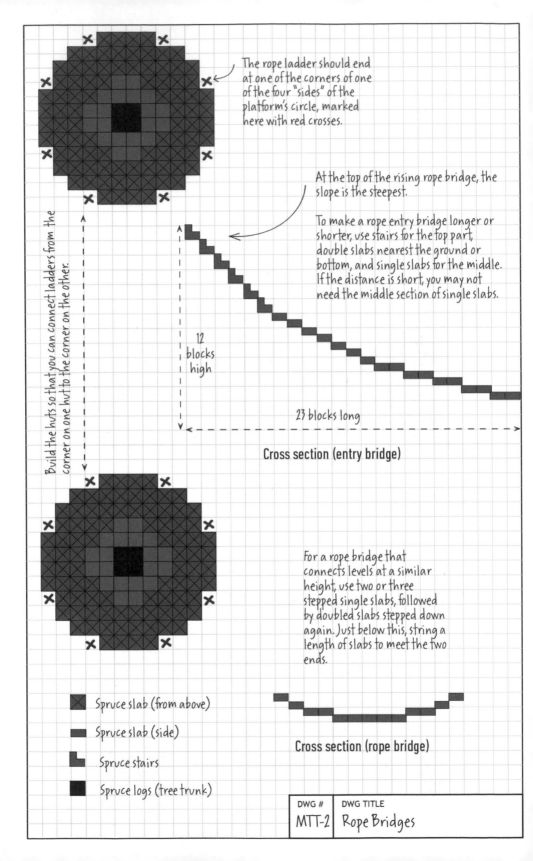

The rope ladder should end at one of the corners of one of the four "sides" of the platform's circle, marked here with red crosses.

At the top of the rising rope bridge, the slope is the steepest.

To make a rope entry bridge longer or shorter, use stairs for the top part, double slabs nearest the ground or bottom, and single slabs for the middle. If the distance is short, you may not need the middle section of single slabs.

12 blocks high

23 blocks long

Cross section (entry bridge)

Build the huts so that you can connect ladders from the corner on one hut to the corner on the other.

For a rope bridge that connects levels at a similar height, use two or three stepped single slabs, followed by doubled slabs stepped down again. Just below this, string a length of slabs to meet the two ends.

Cross section (rope bridge)

- ⊠ Spruce slab (from above)
- ▬ Spruce slab (side)
- ▟ Spruce stairs
- ■ Spruce logs (tree trunk)

DWG #	DWG TITLE
MTT-2	Rope Bridges

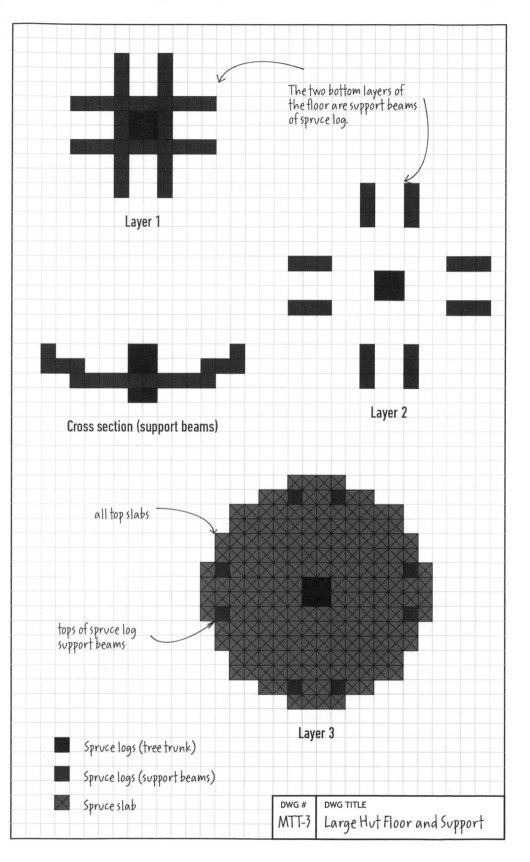

Layer 1

The two bottom layers of the floor are support beams of spruce log.

Layer 2

Cross section (support beams)

Layer 3

all top slabs

tops of spruce log support beams

■ Spruce logs (tree trunk)

■ Spruce logs (support beams)

▨ Spruce slab

DWG #	DWG TITLE
MTT-3	Large Hut Floor and Support

3. Build your large, central hut next. You may want this to be one of the highest huts of your compound and in a central location. Or you may want your compound to grow organically, and string the huts together as you build them. This hut has spruce log support beams beneath the floor. Look at the blueprint MTT-3 at left to build the floor and support beams. The images here show two 3-D views of the support beams.

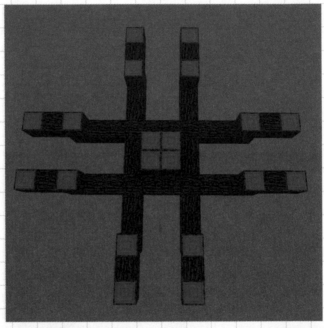

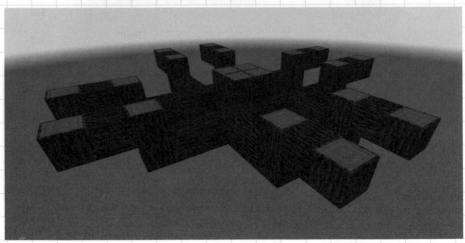

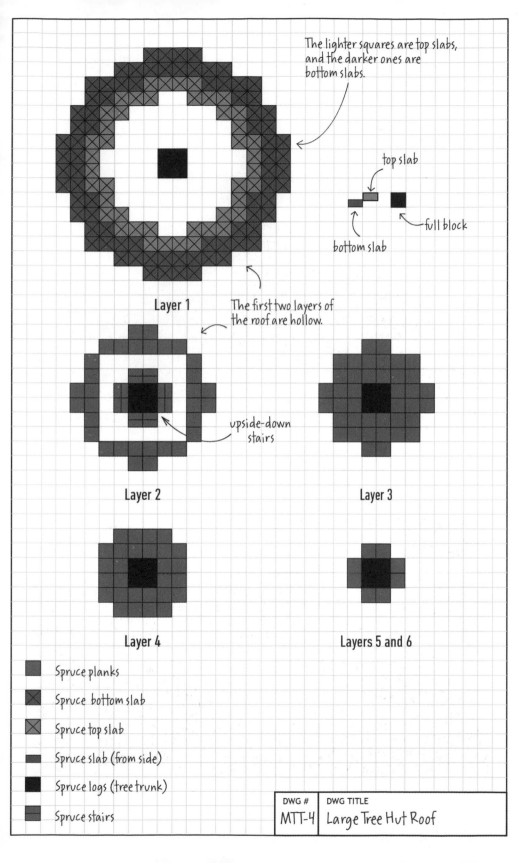

The lighter squares are top slabs, and the darker ones are bottom slabs.

top slab

bottom slab

full block

Layer 1

The first two layers of the roof are hollow.

upside-down stairs

Layer 2

Layer 3

Layer 4

Layers 5 and 6

Spruce planks

Spruce bottom slab

Spruce top slab

Spruce slab (from side)

Spruce logs (tree trunk)

Spruce stairs

DWG #	DWG TITLE
MTT-4	Large Tree Hut Roof

4. Use blueprint MTT-4 on the previous page to build the roof, leaving 4 empty blocks of space between it and the floor platform. As with the small hut, run spruce fence around the sides. Use spruce fence to connect the roof and floor on the outside blocks of the platforms' 4 sides.

5. Add additional huts, at different levels and distances from the large central hut. Connect huts at the same height with rope bridges.

6. Connect huts at differing heights with rising rope bridges, like the rope entry bridge.

7. If the huts are close together, connect them with spruce slab platforms.

"Growing" the Mega Spruce

1. It is likely that you will need to cut down some spruces and plant new trees in the location you want. To make sure your next tree is tall enough, build the main trunk of the tree yourself using 2 x 2 spruce logs.

2. Then, when you want to add the leafy top of the spruce, add a layer of dirt to the trunk, and plant 4 spruce saplings.

3. Use bone meal to grow the top of the tree or wait for growth. Remember to remove the dirt blocks and replace them with spruce logs.

Building Stairs to the Main Hut

4. You can use either stairs (image above, left) or slabs (image above, right) to wind around the main trunk and up to the center of your large hut. You will have to break some of the support blocks to get through to the platform. You can hide this by adding new support beams, if you don't like the way this looks. If you use stairs, you will want to place slabs at each corner to connect the stairs.

CHAPTER 9
WHAT'S NEXT?

CONGRATULATIONS ON BECOMING A MINECRAFT ARCHITECT!

After building these homes, I'm sure you've come up with some ideas of your own for customizing these plans and making them even better! You can customize them to work in different biomes, use different materials, add landscaping, and create new storage buildings and additions. And all the builds are ready for more details, like chairs, tables, and beds inside, and paths and walls outside.

Take screenshots of your buildings from different angles. Once you've set up your shot, press F1 to hide the games interface, or GUI. Then press F2 to take a screenshot. The screenshots will show up in your Minecraft game folder, in a separate folder called "Screenshots."

And if you like the idea of making blueprints of your designs, you can easily make them using square-gridded (quadrille or graph) paper and colored markers and pencils. I've used a dark color for the outlines of each square used and colored the inside with a color that is close to the block used.

Have fun, and share your creations!

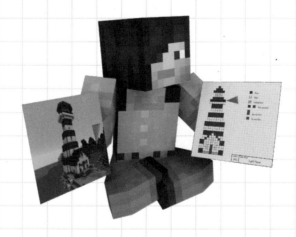